PLANT PARTS

Why Do Plants Have Fruits?

Celeste Bishop

PowerKiDS press.

New York

Published in 2016 by The Rosen Publishing Group, Inc.
29 East 21st Street, New York, NY 10010

First Edition

Editor: Sarah Machajewski
Book Design: Mickey Harmon

Photo Credits: Cover (orange) holbox/Shutterstock.com; cover, p. 1 (logo, frame) Perfect Vectors/Shutterstock.com; cover, pp. 1, 3–4, 7–8, 11–12, 15–16, 19–20, 23–24 (background) djgis/Shutterstock.com; p. 5 Monkey Business Images/Shutterstock.com; p. 6 Mats/Shutterstock.com; p. 9 Dream79/Shutterstock.com; p. 10 Shawn Hempel/Shutterstock.com; p. 13 sta/Shutterstock.com; p. 14 haris M/Shutterstock.com; p. 17 jankamenar.com/Shutterstock.com; p. 18 Jorg Hackemann/Shutterstock.com; p. 21 CreativeNature R.Zwerver/Shutterstock.com; p. 22 (inset) Ekaterina Kondratova/Shutterstock.com; p. 22 (main) tchara/Shutterstock.com.

Library of Congress Cataloging-in-Publication Data

Bishop, Celeste, author.
 Why do plants have fruits? / Celeste Bishop.
    pages cm. — (Plant parts)
 Includes index.
 ISBN 978-1-5081-4217-1 (pbk.)
 ISBN 978-1-5081-4218-8 (6 pack)
 ISBN 978-1-5081-4219-5 (library binding)
 1. Fruit—Juvenile literature. 2. Seeds—Juvenile literature. I. Title.
 QK660.B57 2016
 575.6'7—dc23
                                    2015021397

Manufactured in the United States of America

CPSIA Compliance Information: Batch #BW16PK: For Further Information contact Rosen Publishing, New York, New York at 1-800-237-9932

Contents

What Is a Fruit? 4

Inside and Outside 8

How Many Seeds? 12

Yes, It's a Fruit 16

Colorful and Sweet 19

Eat Fruit, Spread Seeds 20

New Fruits 23

Words to Know 24

Index 24

Websites 24

Do you like to eat fruit?
When you eat it, you're eating
an important plant part.

seeds

A fruit is the part of a plant that holds **seeds**.

The outside of a fruit is called the skin. It can also be called a peel.

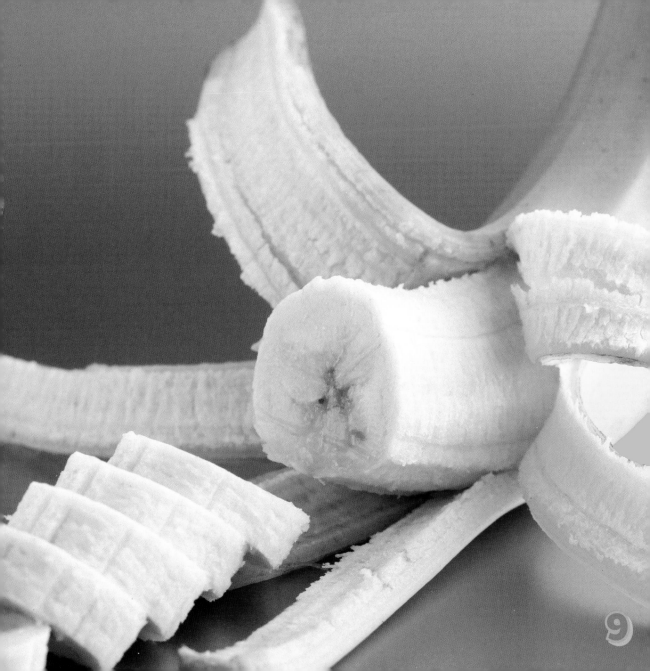

flesh

The soft inside is called the **flesh**. The flesh is where the seeds are.

Some fruits have many seeds.
Apples and bananas have
a lot of tiny seeds.

seeds

Other fruits have only one seed.
Peaches have one big seed.

Some foods are fruit, but they don't look like it. Tomatoes and nuts are fruit because they have seeds.

Fruits are colorful. They're also sweet. This makes people and animals want to eat the fruit.

When animals and people eat fruit, they help spread the seeds. The seeds are used to grow new plants.

Seeds grow into new plants.
Soon, new fruit will grow!

Words to Know

flesh

seed

Index

F
flesh, 10, 11

P
peel, 8

S
seeds, 6, 7, 11, 12, 13, 15, 16, 20, 23
skin, 8

Websites

Due to the changing nature of Internet links, PowerKids Press has developed an online list of websites related to the subject of this book. This site is updated regularly. Please use this link to access the list: www.powerkidslinks.com/part/frut